SPECIAL REPORTS

THE ISRAELI-PALESTINIAN CONFLICT

BY MARCIA AMIDON LUSTED

CONTENT CONSULTANT

Miriam Elman
Associate Professor, Political Science
Maxwell School of Citizenship and Public Affairs
Syracuse University

Essential Library

An Imprint of Abdo Publishing | abdopublishing.com

abdopublishing.com

Published by Abdo Publishing, a division of ABDO, PO Box 398166, Minneapolis,
Minnesota 55439. Copyright © 2018 by Abdo Consulting Group, Inc. International
copyrights reserved in all countries. No part of this book may be reproduced in
any form without written permission from the publisher. Essential Library™ is a
trademark and logo of Abdo Publishing.

Printed in the United States of America, North Mankato, Minnesota
092017
012018

 **THIS BOOK CONTAINS
RECYCLED MATERIALS**

Cover Photos: Derek Brumby/iStockphoto, left; J. Carillet/iStockphoto, right; Frank
Ramspott/iStockphoto, background
Interior Photos: Wojtek Chmielewski/Shutterstock Images, 4–5; Ryan Rodrick Beiler/
Shutterstock Images, 6; Shutterstock Images, 10, 14, 21, 50–51; Golden Brown/
Shutterstock Images, 12; Prisma/Universal Images Group/Getty Images, 16–17;
Bettmann/Getty Images, 19; Time Life Pictures/Mansell/The LIFE Picture Collection/
Getty Images, 26; Universal History Archive/Universal Images Group/Getty Images,
28–29; AP Images, 34, 37, 39, 72–73; iStockphoto, 42–43; Jim Pringle/AP Images,
48, 53; Robert W. Nicholson/National Geographic/Getty Images, 57; Hatem Moussa/
AP Images, 59; Richard T. Nowitz/Corbis Historical/Getty Images, 60–61; Bob
Daugherty/AP Images, 63; Kurt Strumpf/AP Images, 64–65; Muhammed Muheisen/
AP Images, 67; Bride Lane Library/Popperfoto/Getty Images, 76; Max Nash/AP
Images, 79; Yoray Liberman/Getty Images News/Getty Images, 83; Nasser Ishtayeh/
AP Images, 84–85; Bernat Armangue/AP Images, 88–89; Ariel Schalit/AP Images, 93;
NurPhoto/Corbis News/Getty Images, 94–95; Evan Vucci/AP Images, 98

Editor: Arnold Ringstad
Series Designer: Maggie Villaume

Publisher's Cataloging-in-Publication Data

Names: Lusted, Marcia Amidon, author.
Title: The Israeli-Palestinian conflict / by Marcia Amidon Lusted.
Description: Minneapolis, Minnesota : Abdo Publishing, 2018. | Series: Special reports
    | Includes bibliographical references and index.
Identifiers: LCCN 2017946875 | ISBN 9781532113338 (lib.bdg.) | ISBN 9781532152214
    (ebook)
Subjects: LCSH: Middle East--Palestine--Juvenile literature. | Arab-Israeli conflict-
    -Juvenile literature. | Jewish-Arab relations--Juvenile literature.
Classification: DDC 956.04--dc23
LC record available at https://lccn.loc.gov/2017946875

CONTENTS

CHAPTER ONE

JUST ANOTHER DAY

For Israeli woman Rachel Baruch, it is a warm, ordinary day in July 2014. She has chosen to spend it at the beach near Tel Aviv, Israel, enjoying the sunshine and the waters of the Mediterranean Sea. But the peace is soon shattered by rockets, perhaps fired by the Islamic militant group Hamas. Baruch hears a voice call out over loudspeakers, telling people to seek shelter. She begins moving toward a small bomb shelter on the beach. She later recalled what she was thinking:

> There is no way the structure can hold us all, but it is just as well because I'm barely out of the water when the rocket is intercepted and explodes a few blocks from where I am. It is close enough that the ground shakes; I see the light from the explosion, the boom feels loud enough to swallow all the silence I've never heard.[1]

Bomb shelters and the threat of violence are facts of life in modern Israel.

רשות שדות התעופה בישראל
ISRAEL AIRPORTS AUTHORITY
BEN-GURION AIRPORT - נמל התעופה בן־גוריון

מרחב מוגן
SHELTER

The sirens continue to go off over the next few days as more rockets curve overhead. Some are intercepted by Israel's missile defense system, called the Iron Dome. For Israelis, hostile events such as Hamas rocket fire are a way of life, something they must learn to live with. They also must contend with missile attacks from the militant group Hezbollah, as well as terrorist attacks from Palestinian extremists.

THROUGH THE CHECKPOINT

Southeast of Tel Aviv, in the West Bank area of Palestine— referred to by most nations as the Occupied West Bank territory of Palestine, since it is partly under Israeli control—an ordinary day unfolds differently. It is 2:00 a.m.,

Security checkpoints are a part of daily life for many Palestinians.

and Talib Ahmed is waiting to pass through a checkpoint into Israel to work. He is a builder who has been working in Israel for 30 years. Many Palestinians work in Israel because they can make higher wages there. Like many workers who cross national borders, he faces security checks when crossing into the country where he works. The process can take hours. Ahmed explains why he goes through this process:

> I woke up at 1:30 in the morning to get here by 3 a.m. . . . It's cold and dark when I wake up, and the rest of my family is asleep. I do this every morning, five days a week, so I can cross through to work in Israel and make some money to feed my eight children. . . . When I get back, I have an hour or two before I have to sleep, so I can repeat the whole day again. But I thank God. My job pays better than I could make in the West Bank.[2]

OCCUPIED OR NOT?

In territorial disputes, words can be major points of contention. The phrase *occupied territories*, which is frequently used by other countries to refer to the Israeli presence in the West Bank, is an example of this. It technically refers to a country holding territory beyond its official borders, but in the case of Israel, since no borders have been agreed upon through negotiations, it refers to territory beyond the 1949 armistice lines. Many Israelis believe that the occupation is lawful as the territories were captured in a war of self-defense in 1967. Others claim the territories should be considered disputed rather than occupied. The Palestinians argue that the West Bank is under occupation due to the presence of Israeli settlers on land designated for the Palestinian state.

Many Palestinian workers are glad they can earn good wages in Israel. Still, the workers who travel into Israel every day have learned to be very careful. Terror attacks have created tensions, so they don't reach into their pockets in crowded areas in case it looks like they're reaching for a bomb. They don't even carry eating utensils that might be mistaken for weapons.

A COMPLICATED PAST

Israel and Palestine share a small sliver of land sandwiched between the countries of Jordan and Egypt and the Mediterranean Sea. This relatively small area holds the country of Israel as well as the Palestinian territories of the West Bank and the Gaza Strip. Palestine is recognized as a state by approximately 70 percent of the countries in the United Nations (UN), though not by Israel or the United States and its largest allies. Some of the nations that recognize Palestine as a state do not recognize Israel as a state.

Israel was established as a nation in 1948, following World War II (1939–1945). It was created as a homeland for the Jewish people of the world, following agreements in the 1920s that established the legal basis for Israel. Since 1948, there has been an ongoing conflict between Israel and Palestine over land and sovereignty. The conflict has resulted in violence, political strife, multiple wars, and frequent bloodshed.

Each area has its own organizations and government. Israel is ruled by a parliamentary democracy, headed by both a president and a prime minister. Its parliament is called the Knesset. People cannot become citizens of Israel simply by being born there; at least one parent must be Israeli to be a citizen at birth. People can also apply for citizenship as adults. Israeli politics includes multiple political parties. They hold varying opinions and attitudes toward Palestine.

"MY DEFINITION OF A TRAGEDY IS A CLASH BETWEEN RIGHT AND RIGHT. AND IN THIS RESPECT, THE ISRAELI-PALESTINIAN CONFLICT HAS BEEN A TRAGEDY, A CLASH BETWEEN ONE VERY POWERFUL, VERY CONVINCING, VERY PAINFUL CLAIM OVER THIS LAND AND ANOTHER NO LESS POWERFUL, NO LESS CONVINCING CLAIM."[3]

—ISRAELI AUTHOR AMOS OZ

Benjamin Netanyahu, a member of the Likud party, served as prime minister of Israel from 1996 to 1999 and again beginning in 2009.

Palestine's governmental structure is the Palestinian Authority (PA), which elects a president and a legislative council. The PA is controlled by the Fatah party. Fatah is one part of the Palestine Liberation Organization (PLO). The PLO includes political parties, popular organizations, and smaller resistance movements. The 1974 Arab League Summit, a meeting between the leaders of several Arab countries, recognized the PLO as the "sole and legitimate representative of the Palestinian people."[4] Since then, the PLO has represented Palestine at the UN. It supports the movement for a universally recognized independent State of Palestine.

Fatah struggles with another group, Hamas, for political control of Palestine. Hamas is an Arabic acronym that means "Islamic Resistance Movement." The group follows a fundamentalist interpretation of the Sunni branch of Islam. After winning elections in 2006, Hamas violently seized the Gaza Strip from the PA.

THE PLO

The Palestine Liberation Organization (PLO) was founded in 1964 and is the face and voice of the Palestinian national movement. Its structure includes the Palestine National Council (PNC), which is Palestine's equivalent of a parliament. This decision-making body has 124 members. The Executive Committee is made up of 18 members of the PNC and represents the PLO internationally. It also adopts a budget and oversees the functioning of all parts of the PLO. The Central Council mediates between the PNC and the Executive Committee.

A GRIM REALITY

There are no easy answers to the situation in Israel and Palestine. The small slice of land that they occupy is the setting for a confusing and intertwined set of circumstances and issues. Many groups claim to have a historic right to live there. These claims are complicated by religious traditions that are also rooted in this area of

Mahmoud Abbas took office as the president of Palestine in 2008.

the Middle East. Conflicts between Israel and Palestine are made even more complex by the frequent involvement of countries outside the region.

In 2014, Israeli author Einat Wilf and Palestinian university professor Mohammed S. Dajani Daoudi published a joint statement about Israeli-Palestinian

MORE TO THE
STORY

THREE MAJOR RELIGIONS

Israel and Palestine are considered to be holy lands by three major religions: Christianity, Judaism, and Islam. Christianity and the Bible focus on Jerusalem and the surrounding areas because many events in the Bible took place there, including the crucifixion of Jesus. Both Israel and Palestine claim Jerusalem as their capital. The area is sacred to Jews because Jerusalem is the site of Solomon's Temple, also called the First Temple, said to be the source of the foundation stone from which the world was created. The temple was destroyed in 586 BCE and replaced with the Second Temple. One of the remnants of the Second Temple, the Western Wall, is one of Judaism's most holy places to pray. And yet, in 1967, the holiest place in Judaism, the Temple Mount itself, was declared off-limits for worship by Jews and other non-Muslims, though they can visit it.

Jerusalem is the third-holiest site in Islam, since it contains the shrine of the Dome of the Rock and the al-Aqsa Mosque, both located on the Temple Mount, which is known to Muslims as Haram al-Sharif, or the Noble Sanctuary. Muslims believe their religion's founder, the prophet Muhammad, traveled there from Mecca, and that the current mosque holds the stone from which Muhammad ascended into heaven. Following an agreement between Israel and Jordan in 1967, Jews and other non-Muslims are forbidden from praying there.

Many of Israel's cities are found along the Mediterranean coastline.

relations. Coming from both sides of the continuing conflict in their area, they represented the respective viewpoints of their people and the strong opinions about how the lands of Israel and Palestine should be apportioned. Wilf had already been a part of many discussions with Palestinians about questions of sovereignty and statehood. Wilf was asked to write a statement that conveyed what she, as an Israeli, would need to see from the Palestinians to convince her that they wanted to be partners for peace. Then she was contacted by Professor Daoudi. They wrote a new statement:

The Jewish people around the world and Palestinian people around the world are both indigenous to the Land of Israel/ Palestine and therefore have an equal and legitimate right to settle and live anywhere in the Land of Israel/Palestine, but given the desire of both peoples to a sovereign state that would reflect their unique culture and history, we believe in sharing the land between a Jewish state, Israel, and an Arab state, Palestine, that would allow them each to enjoy dignity and sovereignty in their own national home. Neither Israel nor Palestine should be exclusively for the Jewish and Palestinian people respectively and both should accommodate minorities of the other people.[5]

"SOMETIMES I WONDER IF THERE IS ANY HOPE LEFT FOR AN ISRAELI-PALESTINIAN DISCOURSE THAT IS BUILT ON EQUALITY AND LIBERTY."[6]

—ISRAELI-ARAB NOVELIST AND COLUMNIST SAYED KASHUA

Dialogues like this, between two activists working for peace, represent positive steps to bring peace to a part of the world that has long been in conflict. But today, the reality in Israel and Palestine remains one of violence and unease. To understand why the situation is so difficult to resolve, it is necessary to look back in history. The roots of these issues, and of the perspectives of Israelis and Palestinians, date back to biblical times.

CHAPTER TWO

A HOLY
LAND

Jerusalem is among the oldest cities in the world. Its history stretches back to 4000 BCE. Archaeologists have unearthed shards of pottery and ceramics than can be dated to this period, part of what is known as the Copper Age. They have also found evidence that a permanent settlement was located there during the Bronze Age, which lasted from approximately 3000 to 2800 BCE. During the Bronze Age, the development of metalworking techniques allowed civilizations to create new tools, weapons, and other forms of technology, such as the wheel and the plow. This allowed societies to grow quickly, and it was during this time that the first houses and city walls were built in what would become

Historians have built a scale model of what Jerusalem likely looked like in ancient times. The model is at the Israel Museum in Jerusalem.

Jerusalem. Ancient texts and letters also mention a city on that location, called Roshlamem or Rosh-ramen.

A CITY CONQUERED

Almost from its founding, the city of Jerusalem would be fought over repeatedly. This was largely because its location was considered holy by several different religions. Around 1200 BCE, the city was conquered by a tribe called the Canaanites, but by 1000 BCE it was taken over by King David, who declared the city to be the capital of a Jewish kingdom. Stories of King David and his son, King Solomon, are a part of Jewish, Christian, and Islamic religious traditions, and King Solomon was said to have built the First Temple in Jerusalem around 960 BCE. This period of history is referred to as the First Temple Period, when Jerusalem was the capital of first the United Kingdom of Israel, and then the Kingdom of Judah. The temple was the religious center for all the Israelites, the 12 tribes that inhabited Israel.

For the next thousand years, Jerusalem and the surrounding area would be traded back and forth in a series of invasions. Temples and walls were destroyed

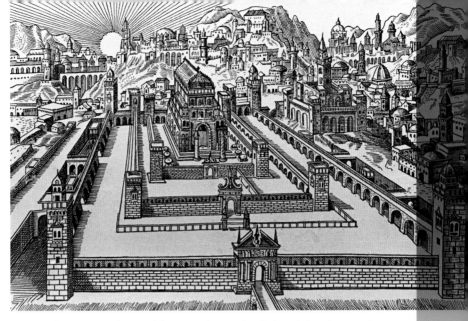

Solomon's Temple stood for several centuries before being destroyed.

and rebuilt as control shifted between the Babylonians, Persians, Greeks, and Romans. The First Temple Period ended when the Babylonian ruler Nebuchadnezzar II, who reigned in the 500s BCE, destroyed the temple Solomon had built. His forces took many Jewish people captive when they revolted against him. Fifty years later, the king of Persia, Cyrus the Great, welcomed the Jews back to Jerusalem to rebuild their temple. The Second Temple was completed 70 years after the First Temple was destroyed. Alexander the Great of Macedonia would then conquer the Persian Empire and take control of Jerusalem and the Kingdom of Judea. The city and the holy land around it were caught up in swirling politics and territorial wars for centuries.

THE ROMANS ARRIVE

Many of the stories about Jerusalem and the Holy
Land that are found in the Christian Bible take place
during the Roman occupation of the city, which began
in approximately 63 BCE. The Roman general Pompey
captured the city for Rome. The Romans installed Herod
the Great as king in 37 BCE. Herod was interested in
making the city beautiful and more useful for commerce.
Many stone walls, towers, and palaces were built during
Herod's era, and he also added to the Temple Mount, the
site of the two Jewish temples, by strengthening it with
walls of stone.

The Romans ruled the growing city of Jerusalem
and its surrounding area. In approximately 30 CE, Jesus,
founder of the Christian religion, was said to have been
crucified in Jerusalem. In 66, the Jews in Jerusalem
revolted against the Romans and took control of the city.
But in 70, the Roman general Titus laid siege to Jerusalem
and destroyed the Second Temple. He banned Jews from
entering the city. The ban lasted for hundreds of years. The
loss of Jerusalem has been mourned for centuries, and this

The Western Wall, a remnant of the Second Temple, is a holy site for the Jewish faith.

mourning over lost land has been incorporated into Jewish traditions and faith practices.

Jerusalem continued to be a pawn in wars between the Roman Empire, the Sassanid Persian Empire, and the Byzantine Empire until the 600s CE. In 638 CE, the Islamic Caliph Omar entered Jerusalem. A caliph was the chief civil and religious leader of the Islamic people, and he was considered to be the direct successor of the Islamic

THE RISE OF ISLAM

Islam is the youngest of the world's major religions. It began in Saudi Arabia in 610 CE, founded by the prophet Muhammad. He is said to have had a vision from an angel, who provided him with the text for the Koran, the holy book of Islam. The angel's dictations of the Koran are considered the perfect words of Allah, or God. Islam is divided into two branches: Shia and Sunni. The Shia believe that only direct descendants of the prophet Muhammad can guide his community, and that their next leader, or caliph, should be his most direct descendant. The Sunni believe that the Prophet's successor should be determined by a consensus, and they elected four caliphs as leaders of the Muslim community. Today, the Shia revere Ali, the first successor of Muhammad, while Sunni revere the four caliphs who were determined to be the Prophet's successors. The difference between the two sects has caused conflicts in worship as well as in religious and political views.

prophet Muhammad. Omar extended his rule to Jerusalem because it was considered to be the third-holiest city in Islam, following Mecca and Medina. Muhammad was said to have ascended to heaven from Jerusalem's Temple Mount. Jerusalem would remain under Arab control until the time of the Crusades.

THE CRUSADES

Initially, while the Arabs controlled Jerusalem, they allowed Jews and Christians to also live there. However, as time went on, new Turkish Arab rulers became less tolerant. They began persecuting Christians and were also a threat to the Byzantine emperor Alexius Comnenus. In the 1090s, the emperor decided to ask the Christian leader in Europe, Pope Urban II, for help. The pope sent out an appeal for a crusade, a religious war supported by the church. The war's aim was to aid the Eastern Christians being persecuted in Jerusalem and to regain the Holy Land from the Islamic rulers and inhabitants. The first Europeans to answer his call were French and German peasants with no military training. But in 1096, a group of 4,000 knights on horseback, along with 25,000 foot soldiers, departed Europe for the Holy Land and Jerusalem.[1]

The crusaders traveled through what is now Turkey and attacked the city of Antioch. They captured it and killed many of the inhabitants, then rested for six months before heading for Jerusalem. By now, the army had only 1,200 knights and 12,000 foot soldiers.[2] In June 1099, they arrived at Jerusalem, but the city's fortifications were so high and strong that it would not be an easy attack. It took many days for the crusaders to build siege towers that would allow them to infiltrate the stone walls. By July 14, the crusaders entered the city and opened the gates to the rest of their army. They began killing all the non-Christian residents of the city, including the Jews. Many Jews barricaded themselves inside synagogues in their section of Jerusalem, but they were often burned out, then captured to be sold into slavery or killed. The crusaders captured Jerusalem and defeated the Islamic armies that attempted to retake the city. The leaders of the First Crusade, as it later became known, set up five small Christian states within the Holy Land, controlling the entire area.

With the crusaders ruling Jerusalem and the Holy Land, it was easier and safer for Christians to travel there. It became popular for people from Europe to make pilgrimages to this area to visit the places described in the Bible. Many Jews returned to the area as well, hoping to resettle in their homeland. Even after the crusaders were ejected by a Muslim army led by the general Saladin in the late 1100s, Jews were still given freedom to live there, though they faced discrimination and sometimes persecution.

OTTOMAN RULE

The Ottoman Empire controlled Jerusalem from 1517, when it captured the region, until 1917. It divided the area into four districts, ruling them from the city of Istanbul in Turkey. The Ottoman government allowed many Jewish people to return to the area or settle there for the first time. The result was a thriving industrial, intellectual, and cultural center. Sultan Suleiman the Magnificent made many improvements to the area, such as reconstructing the old crumbling wall around the city in 1536. But after his death in 1566, the region was neglected, and many of the forests were cut down. Taxes were high and people were poor.

In the 1800s, many foreign powers were interested in Jerusalem and the Holy Land for religious, historical, or academic reasons. The United States, Britain, and France opened schools for biblical history and archaeology. Britain, France, Russia, Austria, and the United States opened diplomatic offices in Jerusalem. With the opening of the Suez Canal, which linked the Mediterranean Sea to the Red Sea in 1869, travel and trade became easier.

Steamships began regular routes to the Holy Land, and roads and telegraph lines were built. New Jewish settlements were constructed, first outside the city walls of Jerusalem, and then in surrounding rural areas. As Jerusalem and the Holy Land were brought into the modern era, nations struggled over who would control this area and who would live there. Two world wars would play major roles in determining the region's future.

Sultan Suleiman the Magnificent ruled the region in the mid-1500s.

CHAPTER THREE

FORMING A
NEW NATION

F our hundred years of Ottoman-Turkish rule in Jerusalem ended in 1917, when the British entered the city during World War I (1914–1918). From January to June of 1919, during the Paris Peace Conference that followed the war, the fate of the Israel-Palestine area was decided by the League of Nations. This international organization was a predecessor to the UN. During this conference, the league created the mandate system. This policy, backed by international law, stated that nations unable to create and maintain their own governments would be overseen by more "advanced nations."[1] The overseers would conduct the affairs of the government until that

The British arrival in Jerusalem would prove to be a turning point in the region's history.

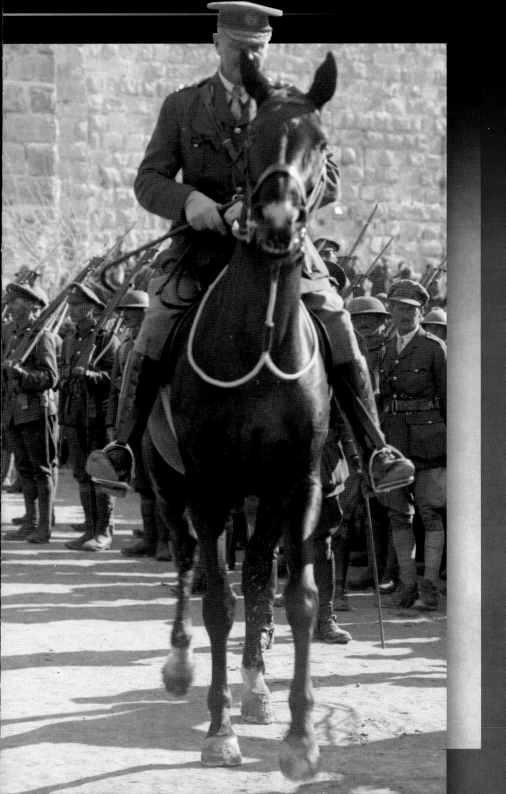

new nation was ready to operate its governmental affairs on its own:

> To those colonies and territories which . . . are inhabited by peoples not yet able to stand by themselves under the strenuous conditions of the modern world, there should be applied the principle that the well-being and development of such peoples form a sacred trust of civilization. . . . The best method of giving practical effect to this principle is that the tutelage of such peoples should be entrusted to advanced nations who by reason of their resources, their experience or their geographical position can best undertake this responsibility, and who are willing to accept it.[2]

LEAGUE OF NATIONS

The League of Nations was created in 1920 following World War I. It was an international organization with headquarters in Switzerland, and its purpose was to provide a forum where countries could resolve their disputes without resorting to war. Even though the idea was put forth by President Woodrow Wilson in 1918 as part of a plan for peace in Europe, opposition in the US Congress meant the United States never became a member of the league. In 1945, the League of Nations was replaced by the United Nations.

Under this new mandate, the members of the League of Nations divided up the former Ottoman territory into new mandates, similar to states. League members such as the United Kingdom and France oversaw these mandates, under the supervision of the League of Nations. These trusts would stay in place until the supervising nations considered the areas ready for self-government.

Under this mandate system, France would oversee Syria and Lebanon. The British were given Iraq and a new entity called Palestine in 1920. In this mandate, Palestine included lands on both sides of the Jordan River, in what is today Israel and Jordan. Jews originally were meant to be able to settle throughout the mandate. However, the British would soon divide the Palestine mandate into two areas. Palestine would be west of the Jordan River. Transjordan, later renamed Jordan, would be east of the river. Jews would not be allowed to settle there. While these two areas were originally covered by the same mandate, eventually the British decided to use a separate government administration for Transjordan.

THE BALFOUR DECLARATION

In 1917, British foreign secretary Arthur James Balfour wrote a letter to the United Kingdom's most famous Jewish citizen and Zionist, Baron Lionel Walter Rothschild. The letter expressed support for the idea of creating a Jewish homeland in Palestine. The letter stated, "His Majesty's Government view with favor the establishment in Palestine of a national home for the Jewish people, and will use their best endeavors to facilitate the achievement of this object, it being clearly understood that nothing shall be done which may prejudice the civil and religious rights of existing non-Jewish communities in Palestine, or the rights and political status enjoyed by Jews in any other country."[3] The letter would influence the British Mandate.

A JEWISH NATIONAL HOME

As part of their governance of the Palestine Mandate, the British supported the creation of a "national home" for the Jewish people. The mandate stated that it was:

> ... in favor of the establishment in Palestine of a national home for the Jewish people, it being clearly understood that nothing should be done which might prejudice the civil and religious rights of existing non-Jewish communities in Palestine, or the rights and political status enjoyed by Jews in any other country.[4]

The mandate would encourage Jewish immigration into the region. It also recognized the World Zionist Organization, an organization that sought to establish a Jewish state in Palestine, as a group that would advise and cooperate with the British administrators.

For those people who had long lived in Palestine and weren't Jewish, the British support of a Jewish homeland in the Palestine Mandate was not well received. The Jews dreamed of settling in self-sufficient farming communities. Many Palestinians lived in the rural countryside, and they protested against the new terms of the mandate. Though the Jewish settlers purchased the lands they settled on, some Palestinians reoccupied lands that had been settled

MORE TO THE
STORY

ZIONISM

Zionism is a movement for Jewish self-determination and the revival of the Jews' national home in their ancient land. The movement initially called for the reestablishment of a Jewish nation in Palestine and now works to develop and protect the nation of Israel. The name *Zionism* comes from the hill Zion, upon which the Temple of Jerusalem was built. Many Jews consider Zionism to be a central part of their religion. The World Zionist Organization was founded in 1897 by Theodor Herzl. In 1896, in a pamphlet called *The Jewish State*, he outlined a plan for Jews to establish a homeland in Palestine:

> The creation of a new State is neither ridiculous nor impossible. . . . We must not imagine the departure of the Jews to be a sudden one. It will be gradual, continuous, and will cover many decades. The poorest will go first to cultivate the soil. In accordance with a preconceived plan, they will construct roads, bridges, railways, and telegraph installations; regulate rivers; and build their own dwellings; their labor will create trade, trade will create markets and markets will attract new settlers, for every man will go voluntarily, at his own expense and his own risk. The labor expended on the land will enhance its value, and the Jews will soon perceive that a new and permanent sphere of operation is opening here for that spirit of enterprise which has heretofore met only with hatred and obloquy [abusive language].[5]

by Jewish immigrants, damaging the immigrants' crops and property and assaulting the settlers themselves. There were riots in cities including Jerusalem. The Jewish people wanted to control the Western Wall, but it was beside the Temple Mount, an Islamic holy site. In riots that took place in 1920 and 1929 in places like Hebron, Jaffa, and Safad,

Major riots took place during the years of British control over the Palestine Mandate.

as well as Jerusalem, nearly 250 Jews and Arabs died.[6] Because the British realized that they couldn't defend the Jews in Hebron well enough, the entire community was uprooted and the residents had to relocate.

The biggest riot, called the Arab Revolt, was sparked by the murder of two Jewish men on April 15, 1936, in the Palestine Mandate. Shortly after, the Jewish community retaliated, and two Arabs were killed. Arab leaders called for a general strike in support of their demand for a national Palestinian government. The British had fanned the flames of the conflict by issuing permits for several thousand new immigrants to settle in Palestinian territory. Palestinian Arabs no longer had any confidence in the British government to represent their interests because the United Kingdom seemed to be leaning toward the Zionist movement. As the riots continued, Arabs attacked British troops and police stations as well as Jewish settlements. Roads, pipelines, and railroads were sabotaged. The British put curfews in place and brought in more British troops from the United Kingdom, Malta, and Egypt. Arabs were arrested and sent to camps or heavily fined. In Jaffa, large sections of the Arab part of the city were demolished.

The strike was finally called off in late 1936, but by then, 275 people were dead and 1,112 were wounded.[7] The British-appointed grand mufti, or leader, of Palestine during this period was Haj Amin al Husseini. Husseini was responsible for instigating riots against Jews.

As a result of the unrest, the British government appointed the Palestine Royal Commission to investigate the causes of the revolt and consider the grievances of both the Jewish and Arab sides of the conflict. The commission issued a 400-page report, which said that these differences could not be resolved. It instead recommended dividing the existing Palestine Mandate into two states, with the smaller area for Jews and the larger one for Arabs. Arabs strongly resisted the idea. They opposed the creation of a Jewish state in the region. The riots continued until September 1939, just as another world war was starting in Europe.

ANOTHER WAR, AND THE END OF A MANDATE

The British wanted to make sure that the Arabs in Palestine remained on their side as another war loomed. As part of

Lord Peel, *center*, headed the Palestine Royal Commission.

maintaining good relations, they issued the White Paper of 1939. This document stated:

> His Majesty's Government therefore now declare unequivocally that it is not part of their policy that Palestine should become a Jewish State. They would indeed regard it as contrary to their obligations to the Arabs under the Mandate, as well as to the assurances which have been given to the Arab people in the past, that the Arab population of Palestine should be made the subjects of a Jewish State against their will.[8]

During World War II, Palestine was relatively quiet. Fewer Jews were immigrating at this time because of Nazi Germany's persecution of Jewish people all over Europe, including the mass murder of Jewish people that was known as the Holocaust. Many Jews could have escaped Europe and survived, but restrictions on immigration prevented them from moving to Palestine. The Nazi regime instead killed them in Europe.

In the war, approximately 21,000 Jews and 8,000 Palestinians from the region enlisted to fight with the British forces.[9] As the war continued and the world learned more about the Nazi treatment of the Jews, public sympathy turned to the Jewish people. Many Jews who had spent time in concentration camps could not return

to their homes in Poland or Germany for fear of being
murdered. Those who did attempt to collect their property
were treated mercilessly. The war's destruction meant
that most of them no longer even had homes to return to.
The United States supported allowing these refugees to
immigrate to Palestine instead.

A group of Arab troops who enlisted during World War II gathered for their
first drill under British officers in December 1940.

The British were finished trying to govern the Palestine Mandate. They turned the problem over to the UN, a new international organization that had been formed in the aftermath of the war to foster cooperation among governments. The UN created a special committee on Palestine. In 1947, the UN proposed that the Palestine Mandate be divided into two separate zones: Palestine for the Arabs, and Israel for the Jews. The Arab leadership rejected this partition plan and launched attacks on the Jews of Palestine. A civil war erupted between the Arabs and the Jews in the region. The British then withdrew from Palestine on May 14, 1948, Israel declared independence, and Arab states in the region launched a war against the newly established Israel. When the fighting finally ended in an Israeli victory ten months later, Israel had not only kept the territory given to it by

COOPERATION AND ORANGES

While many Arabs left Israel during the 1948 war, there were about 160,000 Arabs who remained.[10] Many of them worked on citrus farms, growing oranges. Before the war, the area around the city of Jaffa was home to many orange groves. Jaffa was the center of the citrus industry, and many Arabs worked as packers, moving from farm to farm to pack oranges for shipment. Arabs and Jews built good relationships in the citrus industry, and both earned their living from it, either as orchard owners or workers.

the UN but had also taken over 78 percent of the land in the original mandate.[11] This amounted to more of the territory than the Jewish state would have had if the Arab leadership had accepted the 1947 partition plan. More wars would follow, including the 1956 Sinai Campaign, the Six-Day War in 1967, the 1973 Yom Kippur War, and two Palestinian uprisings known as intifadas.

Israel and Palestine continue to maintain an uneasy coexistence, each seeking a greater claim to a place that both consider to be their birthright and their homeland. Their conflicts have shaped their perspectives on the question of just who should live in this area and who has a greater right to it.

> "WE ARE A GENERATION THAT SETTLES THE LAND, AND WITHOUT THE STEEL HELMET AND THE CANNON'S FIRE WE WILL NOT BE ABLE TO PLANT A TREE AND BUILD A HOME."[12]
>
> —ISRAELI MILITARY LEADER MOSHE DAYAN, 1956

CHAPTER FOUR

THE VIEW
FROM ISRAEL

The conflict over who has the right to live in the lands of Israel, Palestine, and Jerusalem has raged for so many years because each side believes that its perspective on the situation, and its history, is the most important. There are many reasons for the continued conflict and the absence of peace. However, one key reason is that Israelis and Palestinians have clashing narratives.

A HISTORY OF ANTI-SEMITISM

From the perspective of Israelis, their experience with thousands of years of persecution and anti-Semitism is one of their claims to having a Jewish homeland in Israel. Jews have come to believe there is no other place

To Israelis, the nation of Israel represents a return to their historical and traditional homeland.

where they are safe from persecution. Beginning with the era of the Romans, then moving through the Crusades and the Spanish Inquisition and to the pogroms of Russia in the 1800s, Jews have been persecuted, attacked, and killed because of their religious identity. This persecution culminated in the Holocaust of World War II, when Nazi Germany killed approximately six million Jews. Not only was this an immense catastrophe, but for many Jewish people it was also a moment when the world did nothing to help them. They felt that the United States, the United Kingdom, and other nations failed to come to their immediate aid even after they learned about what was happening in Europe under Germany's dictator, Adolf Hitler. Historian William D. Rubenstein notes:

> The list of alleged Allied failures is long, ranging from closing
> their doors to Jewish refugee emigration prior to and during the

POGROMS

Pogrom is a Russian word. It means "to destroy violently." But historically, it has specifically referred to attacks on Jewish people carried out from the 1800s onward in the Russian Empire. Such attacks were usually organized locally, with the approval of local government and police. These attacks occurred because non-Jewish people resented the Jews economically, socially, and politically. They also fed on a long tradition of anti-Semitism. During the pogroms, Jewish people were raped and killed, and their homes and businesses were looted.

Holocaust, forestalling the creation of a Jewish state in Palestine

when this was most necessary as a place of refuge, failing to

bomb Auschwitz or any other death camp, failing to engage

in negotiations with the Nazis with the aim of bartering for

Jewish life and failing, until early 1944, to create any specialised

government agency to save Jewish lives, oblivious to the fact

that Hitler was engaged in a 'war against the Jews.'[1]

As a result of the genocide carried out against Jewish people, Israelis feel that they have the right to a safe, protected homeland in Israel. Sympathy for what the Jewish people endured during the Holocaust was a motivating factor in the UN recognition of Israel.

However, perhaps the strongest overall reason that Jews feel they should live in Israel is that they have a right to a sovereign country of their own, located in their ancient homeland. Claiming that their right to live in Israel is justified by their history of persecution is only part of the story. Like many people all over the world, the Israelis feel it is important to live in the land where their ancestors did.

Israelis believe that they have a right to their land because it was the birthplace of the Jewish people. According to Israel's Ministry of Foreign Affairs, Israel's history begins 3,700 years ago, when the biblical figure

Moses led his people away from Egypt, where they were used as slaves by the Egyptian pharaohs. Moses brought the Jews out of Egypt to the land of Israel, which the people believed had been promised to them by God and by their forefathers. The Jewish people were united by King David, who ruled Jerusalem and Israel until a series of invaders and rulers took it away from them. They feel their bond with the area has never broken, despite wars and displacement. They point to the fact that except when Jews have been forcefully expelled, they have lived in the area continuously.

A SAFE HAVEN AT LAST

For the Jewish people, May 14, 1948, was the day when they finally achieved a secure homeland, a refuge and a safe harbor from anti-Semitism and

ARAB OR NOT?

Part of Israel's claim to the area is that Palestine was never an exclusively Arab area. When large numbers of Jews began to immigrate to Palestine in 1882, the area was only sparsely populated. The land was swampy, and diseases like malaria were common, making it nearly uninhabitable. There were fewer than 250,000 Arabs there, and many of them had only lived there for a few decades.[2] Israelis claim that because there was never an independent state of Palestine there, Israel's presence in the West Bank is not illegal. Rather, many Israelis and their supporters insist that Jews have a legal right to live in this area as established by international consensus and international law dating back to the 1920s.

persecution. This was the day when Israel declared itself a state. Soon afterward, both the United States and the Soviet Union officially recognized the new nation. The Jewish People's Council gathered in Tel Aviv and wrote a document called the Declaration of the Establishment of the State of Israel, which reads:

THE STATE OF ISRAEL will be open for Jewish immigration and for the Ingathering of the Exiles; it will foster the development of the country for the benefit of all its inhabitants; it will be based on freedom, justice and peace as envisaged by the prophets of Israel; it will ensure complete equality of social and political rights to all its inhabitants irrespective of religion, race or sex; it will guarantee freedom of religion, conscience, language, education and culture; it will safeguard the Holy Places of all religions; and it will be faithful to the principles of the Charter of the United Nations.[3]

With the establishment of the state of Israel, even Jews who had never set foot in Israel would have a safe place to go if another wave of persecution happened. The Israeli Law of Return, enacted in 1950, states that any Jewish person in the world can immigrate to Israel and become a citizen. Because it is so important to them to have this safety, Israelis feel they must remain strong and

vigilant to preserve their state and maintain its security against enemies that might try to destroy it.

Israel's parliament passed a law stating that the State of Israel belongs to all Jewish people—not just those who are citizens there, but also all Jews, all over the world. While only citizens of Israel can elect the government and participate in the nation's democracy, Israel was created for the benefit of all Jews everywhere. This fits with the Law of Return, which opens Israel and Israeli citizenship to any Jewish person anywhere.

The Israelis had found their homeland, a place they felt they had an ancestral and religious right to occupy, and they would do what they had to in order to keep their safe haven. But the Palestinian perspective on this series of events was dramatically different.

EXPELLED

Following the creation of Israel, between the 1940s and the 1960s, more than 900,000 Jews were violently expelled or forced to migrate from Arab countries as a result of discriminatory policies.[4] They left Lebanon, Egypt, and other nations, and many fled to Israel. The refugees were not compensated for their loss of property, and their plight has seen little recognition.

Large numbers of Jewish immigrants, including children of European Jews killed during World War II, arrived in the state of Israel in the late 1940s.

CHAPTER FIVE

THE VIEW FROM PALESTINE

In 1947, the UN recommended dividing the British Mandate of Palestine into two states, one for Jews and one for Arabs. While the Jewish people accepted the proposed partition of the land, Arabs felt that it did not fairly represent the way in which Arabs and Jews were distributed across the land of Palestine, and they rejected it. In 1948, Israel was created, but the surrounding Arab nations began fighting Israel once British forces left the area. Israelis called this conflict the War of Independence. The Palestinians referred to it as al-Nakba, or "the Catastrophe." Approximately 750,000 Palestinians were forced to leave what had been British Palestine, driven out or fleeing in fear. Some Arab leaders promised they could return once Israel

Arabs in Palestine feel they have been treated unjustly and unfairly since the creation of Israel.

was destroyed. In some areas, Palestinians were forcibly expelled from their villages, though this was not an official policy of the Israeli government. Israel went on to control large amounts of land and destroy approximately 450 Palestinian villages.[1] Palestinian areas fell under the control of their Arab allies. The Palestinian area of the Gaza Strip was controlled by Egypt, and the Palestinian area of the West Bank was controlled by Jordan. Israel and Jordan split control of the city of Jerusalem. Jordan refused to allow any Israelis—even those who were Muslim or Christian—to visit holy sites in east Jerusalem or the West Bank.

By 1948, Palestinians had not only lost a great deal of land, but they also lacked

RESOLUTION 194

As conflict raged between Arabs and Israelis in 1948, the UN committee working on behalf of Palestinian refugees passed Resolution 194. The resolution states that

> . . . refugees wishing to return to their homes and live at peace with their neighbours should be permitted to do so at the earliest practicable date, and that compensation should be paid for the property of those choosing not to return and for loss of or damage to property which, under principles of international law or equity, should be made good by the Governments or authorities responsible.[2]

The resolution is often taken to mean that there is an actual international law about the right of return, but the intent of the resolution was to propose a solution for peace. No current law exists, and the resolution is a source of contention because Arabs interpret it as permitting the right of return for Palestinian refugees, while Israel interprets it as a matter to be decided via direct negotiations.

a state of their own. As a result of the events of 1948, Palestinians felt as though they had no home. Many of the new citizens of Israel had immigrated to Palestine from Europe, and Palestinians felt the newcomers' bond with Palestine was based only on a religious connection, not a historical one. In 1882, there were 24,000 Jews living in Palestine, making up approximately 5 or 6 percent of the total population. By 1948, there were 650,000 Jews in Palestine, comprising one-third of the population. The remaining two-thirds consisted of Arab Palestinians who were natives of the country.[3] To the Palestinians, it seemed unfair that this group of immigrants was granted a state of

Violence in the late 1940s led to many Arabs becoming refugees.

its own while the Arabs lost not only their country but also, since they lacked a government, their right to decide their future. To Palestinians, this was not logical.

The Palestinians did not approve of the creation of Israel. They disliked that many Arab Palestinians would now have to live within a Jewish state. Some felt it would have made more sense to create one state for all citizens. Before 1948, some Jewish groups supported this model too. However, anti-Jewish violence led many to eventually reject the plan.

VIEWS ON THE HOLOCAUST

Palestinians also feel that they are victims, being punished for Europe's injustice to the Jews. Palestinians have varying views on the Holocaust. Some don't believe that it actually happened and that it is mostly a hoax. Others think it happened, but perhaps not to the degree that historians say. Still others agree with historians that it was a real, horrible instance of genocide.

Some feel it is unfair to use the Holocaust as a way to justify displacing the Palestinian people. They think using such a horrific event as a point of comparison makes

MORE TO THE
STORY

THE HOLOCAUST

Carried out by Germany's Nazi regime, which came to power in 1933, the Holocaust was the systematic, government-sponsored persecution and murder of six million Jews. The Nazis believed that Germans were racially superior and that the inferior Jewish race was a threat to Germans' racial purity. The Nazis also targeted other groups that they considered to be racially inferior, including Roma (gypsies), disabled people, homosexuals, Communists, Socialists, and Jehovah's Witnesses. Some people from Russia, Poland, and other Slavic countries were also targeted. One of the biggest aspects of this persecution involved concentration camps, established by the Nazis in 1933. They were camps with intensely harsh conditions where people were confined, without the usual acceptable legal rules pertaining to arrest and imprisonment. Most prisoners were malnourished. Prisoners were used for forced labor, often for constructing or expanding the camps themselves. After the outbreak of World War II in 1939, the Nazis increasingly used extermination camps, facilities created specifically for murdering large numbers of people rather than imprisoning them.

their own plight seem unimportant. They fear that when Israeli schoolchildren are told that Palestine does not exist, the Arab culture is being erased in the same way the Nazi regime tried to erase Jewish culture, even if the circumstances are much different.

THE NEW CRUSADES?

Palestinians sometimes also see the Israeli conflict as a new version of the Crusades, when European Christians of the Middle Ages attempted to seize control of the Holy Land. Many see the presence of Jews and the Christian support of Israel as being yet another attempt to take Arab lands. This is specifically mentioned in the charter of the Palestinian militant group Hamas:

> The Islamic Resistance Movement views seriously the defeat of the Crusaders . . . and the rescuing of Palestine from their hands. . . . The Movement draws lessons and examples from all this. The present Zionist onslaught has also been preceded by Crusading raids from the West and other Tatar raids from the East. Just as the Moslems faced those raids and planned fighting and defeating them, they should be able to confront the Zionist invasion and defeat it.[4]

The violent legacy of the Crusades factors into some people's feelings about the modern conflicts in the Middle East.

Some Palestinians feel their defeat of the Christian forces during the Crusades is not just a glorious moment in their history, but also a road map for how they can defeat the Zionist movement that created Israel and deprived them of much of their homeland. Israelis argue, in response, that their creation of a Jewish state cannot be compared to the Crusades because, unlike the European Christians of medieval times, Israelis have an ancestral right to Palestine.

Many Palestinians, as well as some Arabs and Muslims globally, view the Jewish presence in the land as sacrilegious. They see the conflict as a holy war and not a dispute over territory. To them, Jews are unbelievers taking over sacred Muslim lands.

IDENTITY AND RETURN

Israelis see themselves as people struggling for land that is their birthright. Palestinians feel they are the victims in the struggle and are trying to survive Israeli aggression toward them. It is also still very important to Palestinians that they have the right of return to the land of Palestine. This would allow refugees to return to the places from which they were displaced.

Most Palestinians who were displaced in 1948 are no longer alive. However, under a unique arrangement that applies only to Palestinian refugees, the UN determined that refugee status could be inherited. Thus today there are nearly 5 million Palestinian refugees. Not all wish to move to Israel. Many would prefer to receive full citizenship rights where they currently live.

Israelis exercise a right of return. This is a large source of contention for Palestinians, who cannot understand why a people who never lived in Israel before can be invited to return by the state of Israel, whereas Palestinians who actually lived in Palestine are forbidden to return to their villages. Palestinians feel it is just one more method Israelis use to remove them from their lands.

Both Israelis and Palestinians have strong feelings and perspectives about each other and about who has the right to occupy land in Palestine and Israel. It makes the conflict difficult to resolve, because it is about much more than just rights to land. It is about the identity of the peoples involved. The situation is further complicated by the involvement of many other countries in the conflict. Since 1948, Palestine and Israel have been at the center of many international attempts to resolve their differences.

In large protests, many Palestinians continue to express frustration and anger about their situation.

CHAPTER SIX

INTERNATIONAL
INVOLVEMENT

There are several reasons why other countries want to see peace in Israel and Palestine. This area of the world is important to many people. The region's status as sacred ground for three major religions, with holy sites associated with each religion, makes it more complicated than just fighting over natural resources or political advantages. If people consider an area to be holy, then their feelings toward it can become more emotional and less rational. For decades, nations around the world have attempted to intervene and calm the region's tensions. These efforts have had varying degrees of success.

Several US presidents, including Bill Clinton in 1993, have tried to broker peace agreements between Israel and Palestine.

THE CAMP DAVID ACCORDS

One of the first concentrated efforts to bring peace in Israel occurred under President Jimmy Carter in the 1970s. Since Israel was established in 1948, it had been in an almost constant state of war with Egypt. Israel had defeated Egypt in three wars and had occupied Egypt's Sinai Peninsula, which links Africa and Asia. When Anwar el-Sadat became the Egyptian president in 1970, he wanted to make peace with Israel to help Egypt recover the Sinai Peninsula and become more stable. He communicated with the United States to help with diplomacy between Egypt and Israel, but then Egypt and Syria launched yet another war against Israel in 1973, known as the Yom Kippur War. Yom Kippur is one of the holiest days in the Jewish year, and Israeli forces were taken by surprise. Israel won the war in a matter of weeks, but Sadat gained more prestige in the Middle East for having made as much progress against Israel as he did. Sadat was now more willing to seek peace, hoping that Egypt could regain land in the Sinai Peninsula. He traveled to the United States in 1975 to discuss peace efforts and

Egyptian president Sadat, *left*, Carter, *center*, and Israeli prime minister Begin, *right*, signed a peace treaty at the White House in 1979.

ask for US aid and money. In September 1978, Carter invited Sadat and Israel's prime minister, Menachem Begin, to the presidential retreat at Camp David in Maryland. There, on September 17, 1978, the Camp David Accords were signed. The agreement said that Israel would completely withdraw from the Sinai Peninsula. On March 29, 1979, the countries' leaders signed a permanent treaty to end the state of war between Israel and Egypt and hopefully pave the way for achieving peace in the Middle East.

FROM THE
HEADLINES

THE BLACK
SEPTEMBER GROUP

Despite the attempts at creating peace under
President Carter, there were still incidents of
violence and terrorism associated with the
continuing conflict. During the 1972 Summer
Olympic Games in Munich, Germany, a Palestinian
group called the Black September Organization
took hostage, tortured, and eventually killed
11 members of the Israeli Olympic team, as
well as a West German police officer. Black
September initially demanded the release of
220 Palestinian prisoners in Israeli and West
German jails, as well as transportation
out of Germany. But when shooting

began between the Black September group and police, all 11 Israeli hostages were murdered.[1]

Black September was organized under the Revolutionary Council of al-Fatah, the PLO's military force. The group formed to seek revenge on the military of Jordan and to assassinate Jordan's King Hussein after a forceful confrontation between that country and the PLO in 1970. The group's name was a reference to that confrontation, which took place in September 1970 and resulted in the deaths or expulsions of thousands of Palestinians from Jordan. The group also carried out attacks against Israeli and Western targets around the world, including acts of terrorism and airplane hijacks. Its first act of violence took place in 1971, when it assassinated Jordan's prime minister, Wasif al-Tali. Al-Tali was believed to have been personally responsible for the torture and death of the Palestinian leader Abu Ali Iyad. The PLO dissolved Black September in 1974, but terror attacks from other groups against Israeli citizens continued through the 1970s and 1980s.

Images of the masked perpetrators became forever linked to the memory of the Munich Olympics.

THE OSLO ACCORDS

President Bill Clinton played a role in the next round of
Israeli-Palestinian peace talks. On September 13, 1993, at
the White House in Washington, DC, Israeli prime minister
Yitzhak Rabin and PLO negotiator Mahmoud Abbas signed
the Declaration of Principles on Interim Self-Government
Arrangements, commonly called the Oslo Accords. In
it, Israel agreed to recognize the PLO as the Palestinian
representative, and the PLO agreed to cease terrorism and
recognize Israel's right to exist as a state in peace. They
both agreed to the formation of a Palestinian Authority,
which was created in 1994 according to the Declaration of
Principles to govern the West Bank and Gaza Strip.

However, the fragile peace fell apart because of
continued terrorism and settlement building. Settlement
building was not forbidden under the Oslo Accords, but
Palestinians saw it as breaking the spirit of the agreements.
Following the assassination of Rabin in 1995 by Yigal Amir,
an Israeli extremist, further peace talks faltered.

Another round of peace talks during the summer of
2000 failed because Israel and Palestine could not agree

about borders, who would control Jerusalem, and the guarantee that Palestinians would have the right of return to go back to Palestine. Another major factor was that the two sides could not come to an agreement on how to share the Temple Mount.

Many commentators claimed that Israel made far-reaching concessions at these talks. They fault Palestinian leader Yasser Arafat for walking away from a generous offer. Others argue that the deal could have been improved and that Arafat was right not to agree to it.

A ROAD MAP FOR PEACE

US president George W. Bush tried to negotiate a peace settlement in 2003. The plan started in 2001 and was created by four political entities: the United States, the European Union, Russia, and the UN. As part of the plan,

President Bush met with Abbas in the West Bank in 2008.

President Bush made a statement calling for Palestine to have its own state, the first time a US president had said this. The plan called for three steps.

In the first, both sides would issue statements supporting a two-state solution, the Palestinians would renounce violence and create a constitution for themselves, and the Israelis would stop settlement activities. In the second phase, an international conference would create a Palestinian state with provisional borders. In the third phase, there would be talks to finalize the agreement. The three phases were never fully implemented, but President Bush tried again in 2007, hosting Israeli prime minister Ehud Olmert and Palestinian Authority president Abbas, as well as representatives of the same four political entities. Some analysts have noted that in 2008, Olmert offered concessions in secret negotiations, but Abbas did not accept the deal.

LEAVING THE GAZA STRIP

In 2003, because of the expense and difficulty in providing security to 8,000 Israeli Jews in Gaza, and in the hope that withdrawals would improve the chances for peace, Israeli prime minister Ariel Sharon announced a disengagement plan, which included removing Israeli settlers from the Gaza Strip and parts of the West Bank:

> Israel will evacuate the Gaza Strip, including all existing Israeli towns and villages, and will redeploy outside the Strip. . . . Upon completion of this process, there shall no longer be any permanent presence of Israeli security forces or Israeli civilians in the areas of Gaza Strip territory which have been evacuated. As a result, there will be no basis for claiming that the Gaza Strip is occupied territory.[2]

The plan was carried out in 2005. While the intent of Sharon's plan was to defuse some of the conflict between Israelis and Palestinians, the Palestinians claimed that it was a result of their violent resistance to Israeli occupation. The Gaza disengagement was supported by a majority of the Israeli public, but

FEELINGS OF PERSECUTION

Many of the Israeli settlers who were removed from the Gaza Strip felt their treatment was similar to the persecution of the World War II era. Some emphasized this point when they were forced to evacuate. An account in the *New York Times* read:

> In one house, a settler who had thrown eggs at soldiers and journalists was one of the last to go. His door had a poster from the Nazi era, implying that Israel was making Gaza a "Jewish-free" zone. He wore an orange Star of David on his shirt, marked "Jude," German for Jew. When his wife finally agreed to leave the house, all her children left with their arms up, screaming in unison, all wearing an orange star, a piece of theater for the television cameras.[3]

many who had lived in the area for nearly four decades were traumatized at being forced to leave their homes, and some had to be dragged from their homes during the disengagement.

NEW TALKS

Peace initiatives begun by President Bush and the four political entities came to an end when Hamas launched a military offensive against Israel in 2008. President Barack Obama tried to restart the peace process in 2009. He persuaded Israeli prime minister Benjamin Netanyahu to put in place a ten-month freeze on the construction of new Israeli settlements in the West Bank, which Netanyahu called "the first meaningful step toward peace."[4] Talks began in

September 2010 between President Abbas, Prime Minister Netanyahu, President Hosni Mubarak of Egypt, and King Abdullah of Jordan, but the negotiations failed and the freeze expired. Some analysts accused Abbas of not taking advantage of the freeze and instead avoiding moving forward with negotiations.

In May 2017, newly elected president Donald Trump met with President Abbas in the White House, saying he would work as a "mediator, an arbitrator or a facilitator" to help bring peace between the Israelis and Palestinians. "We will get this done," Trump said.[6] Two months earlier, when Prime Minister Netanyahu visited the White House, Trump had urged him to hold back on allowing the construction of new settlements in Palestinian territory.

However, tensions continue, including conflict in Jerusalem over the Temple Mount and its status as a holy place for Muslims and Jews. While other countries, including the United States, try to encourage peace in the area, the specter of more violence is always present.

CHAPTER SEVEN

WAR, TERRORISM, AND SECURITY

Israel, Palestine, and neighboring Arab states have experienced many wars since the creation of Israel in 1948. These include the initial war between Jewish and Arab militias in 1948 and 1949 following the end of the British Mandate. This conflict resulted in a set of agreements between Israel, Egypt, Jordan, Lebanon, and Syria, called the 1949 Armistice Agreements, which established the boundary lines between Israel and its neighbors. However, fighting continued through the 1950s and 1960s as Israeli forces constantly repelled and retaliated against Arab guerillas who attacked Israeli citizens and soldiers.

Israeli forces emerged victorious at the end of the 1948–1949 war.

The Suez Crisis followed in 1956, when the United Kingdom, France, and Israel attacked Egypt in order to take over control of the Suez Canal, which the Egyptian government had seized a few months earlier. June 1967 saw the Six-Day War between Israel and its Arab neighbors Egypt, Jordan, and Syria. Other nations including Iraq, Saudi Arabia, and Kuwait also sent troops and weapons to the Arab forces. After the war, the territory held by Israel increased to include the West Bank and East Jerusalem, the Golan Heights, the Sinai Peninsula, and the Gaza Strip.

Following the Six-Day War, Israel offered to return the Sinai Peninsula and other territory in exchange for peace. However, any expectations for a new peace process fell flat. On September 1, 1967, 13 Arab states held a meeting in Khartoum, Sudan, and issued the Khartoum Declaration.

THE SIX-DAY WAR

The Six-Day War was marked by aggressive actions on the part of Egypt, Jordan, and Syria in an attempt to eliminate Israel. Egypt massed its troops on the Israeli border and blockaded its southern port, and the Arab states promised to destroy the country of Israel completely. Israelis felt that there was the possibility of another Holocaust and the potential for tens of thousands of deaths. They dug mass graves in public parks and built bunkers, expecting huge numbers of casualties and possible invasion. Israeli military leader Yitzhak Rabin suffered a nervous breakdown from the pressure of the war. Many Israelis still feel, 50 years later, that their victory in the war was nothing short of a miracle.

Egyptian president Gamal Abdel Nasser said of the conflict with Israel, "We shall never surrender and shall not accept any peace that means surrender."[1] This influenced the Arab leaders to issue their infamous "3 No's": no peace with Israel, no negotiations with Israel, no recognition of Israel, and "maintenance of the rights of the Palestinian people in their nation" as specific conditions for peace.[2]

The Arab efforts to recapture lost territory continued with the October 1973 Yom Kippur War, which started with a surprise joint attack on Israel by Egypt and Syria on the Jewish holy day of Yom Kippur. Still, no major territory changes resulted, and Israel defeated the Arab forces.

From 1971 to 1982, the PLO moved into South Lebanon, establishing its base of operations there and carrying out attacks on Israel. To retaliate, in 1978 Israel launched a large-scale invasion of Lebanon, named Operation Litani after Lebanon's Litani River. Its purpose was for the Israeli Defense Forces (IDF) to chase the PLO out of Lebanon. However, as the ground fighting and rocket attacks continued between Israel and the PLO, it escalated into the 1982 Lebanon War. This war was sparked by an assassination attempt against Israel's ambassador to

Egyptian troops planted their flag at the Suez Canal during the
Yom Kippur War.

the United Kingdom, and by the continuing terror attacks

on northern Israel by the PLO and guerilla organizations.

The war succeeded in dislodging the PLO from Lebanon,

and it also resulted in the creation of an Israeli Security

Zone in southern Lebanon. This zone was intended to

protect Israel from violence by the Islamic militant group

Hezbollah and other militant organizations based in Lebanon. This strip of land would stretch across the border between Israel and Lebanon, and it was to be controlled by the UN Interim Force in Lebanon (UNIFIL). But the establishment of the security zone did not end conflicts between the Israelis and Lebanese Muslim guerillas, led by Hezbollah. Fifteen years of conflict would lead to the two bloody intifadas between Palestine and Israel.

SHAKING OFF

The Arabic word *intifada* means "the act of shaking off," but it has come to mean an uprising or rebellion. Specifically, it usually refers to an armed uprising of Palestinians against Israeli occupation of the West Bank and Gaza Strip. The First Intifada, which began in December 1987, was sparked by an Israeli truck crashing into a station wagon that was carrying Palestinian workers in the Gaza Strip. Four were killed and ten were wounded. Palestinians saw the act not as an accident, but as retaliation by the Israelis for the killing of a Jew in Gaza several days earlier. On December 9, 1987, Palestinians took to the streets, throwing rocks, burning tires, and hurling makeshift firebombs at Israeli troops and police. The next day, an Israeli military patrol vehicle fired on Palestinian attackers, killing a teenager and wounding 16 others.[3] The First Intifada had begun.

The First Intifada was a grassroots uprising, meaning that it was started and carried out by regular Palestinian people from all walks of life, not by the military or the PLO. It would soon be commanded by Palestinian leaders, but the intifada was carried out by people from every part of Palestinian society, from schoolchildren to women's groups to affluent Palestinians. In addition to violence, the people used boycotts and strikes against Israelis.

The First Intifada lasted for five years, during which time more than 3,000 Palestinians and 900 Israelis were killed.[4] The intifada ended when peace negotiations began between PLO leader Yasser Arafat and Israeli leader Yitzhak Rabin. In 1994, Arafat, Rabin, and Israeli foreign minister Shimon Peres were jointly awarded a Nobel Peace Prize. Rabin was assassinated in 1995 during a peace rally in Tel Aviv, and the peace process stalled again.

From 1995 to 2002, Israel withdrew the IDF from West Bank cities to comply with the Oslo Accords. This left the

During the First Intifada, Israeli troops faced down Palestinian demonstrators who hurled rocks and bottles at them.

area open to terrorist groups. After a series of mass suicide bombing attacks, the IDF returned to the area in 2002 and succeeded in preventing Hamas, Islamic Jihad, and other terrorist groups from gaining a foothold and spreading even more violence. Israel and the Palestinian Authority, coordinating their efforts, have been able to maintain security and prevent these groups from taking over.

THE SECOND INTIFADA

On September 28, 2000, Israeli politician Ariel Sharon walked onto Jerusalem's Temple Mount, accompanied by media and a security detail. Sharon's action was almost guaranteed to provoke an angry response from

Palestinians, though the PA had coordinated his visit. Sharon's visit was the trigger for a campaign of violence, in part because even though Jews have been able to visit the Temple Mount, Judaism's holiest site, since 1967, many Palestinians nonetheless believe they should not be allowed there. Some Muslim religious leaders called on their followers to attack the Jews for visiting the Temple Mount. This led to riots. The Palestinians who were guarding the area began fighting with Sharon's security force. Seven Palestinians were killed, and the Second Intifada began. The intifada soon spread across Palestine and into Israel. Hamas declared that October 6, 2000, would be a "day of rage" and urged Palestinians to attack Israeli army outposts in the occupied territories.[5] The Second Intifada ended in 2005. Thousands died from suicide bombings, gunfire, tank and air attacks, and violence in response to demonstrations.

However, the conflicts between Israel and the Palestinians were not over. Another war with Lebanon took place in 2006 between Hezbollah forces and the Israeli military. It began when Hezbollah kidnapped Israeli soldiers. The UN helped bring about a cease-fire in August

2006. The three-week Gaza War took place in 2008–2009 between Israel and Hamas, after Israel conducted a surprise air strike against terrorist bases in response to continued rocket fire from the Gaza Strip. Hamas placed its forces in civilian areas, using innocent people as human shields. As a result, civilians sometimes died. Israel ended the conflict in January 2009 and withdrew from Gaza. More conflicts took place in 2012 and 2014.

THE IDF

The Israel Defense Forces (IDF) are Israel's military. According to the Israel Ministry of Foreign Affairs, "The IDF's security objectives are to defend the sovereignty and territorial integrity of the State of Israel, deter all enemies, and curb all forms of terrorism that threaten daily life."[6] It consists of a small standing army, navy, and air force. Its soldiers are drawn from Israeli citizens, who are drafted at the age of 18. In addition to Jewish service members, many Israeli Muslims and Christians serve in the IDF. Women serve for two years and men serve for three years. There are also reserve troops and career military personnel. Noncitizens can volunteer for service in the IDF. The IDF prides itself on being highly trained and equipped with the latest weapons.

Some in Palestinian society glorify terrorism and terrorists. There are monuments to terrorists, and people are paid as an incentive to commit acts of terror against Israelis. Israel's position is that such incitement to violence is a major reason why peace has remained elusive.

FROM THE
HEADLINES

MOHAMMED AL-DURRAH

One of the most memorable, and most controversial, images of the Second Intifada occurred during fighting in the Gaza Strip on September 30, 2000. A French television network was shooting footage of a gun battle between Palestinians and Israelis. The camera fixes on a man named Jamal al-Durrah, who is taking cover against a wall and is not involved in the fighting. He is trying to protect his young son Mohammed from the gunfire. Mohammed is apparently hit by gunfire and collapses. Images of this event were broadcast around the world.

The footage came to represent Palestine's grievances against both Israel and US support of Israel. However, almost immediately after the video was broadcast all over the world, some people cast doubts on whether it truly showed what it was said to show. Israel has said that the incident could not have taken place as it was reported and that the shots could not have been fired by Israeli soldiers. After an investigation by the Israeli government in 2013, the investigators declared that the incident was staged and the boy was not even injured in the incident. The cameraman who filmed the incident was accused of lying in his statements

Media coverage of the Second Intifada played an important role in public discussions of the uprising.

concerning the boy's death, and investigators said that footage showing the boy as apparently uninjured after the incident was eliminated from the footage release. Palestinians, however, maintain that Israeli soldiers were responsible for the boy's death. They continue to use the image as an iconic example of Israel's treatment of Arabs.

SETTLEMENTS

One of the sources of conflict between Israel and Palestine is the issue of Jewish settlements beyond the 1949 armistice lines. After the Six-Day War in 1967, Israel annexed or occupied land in East Jerusalem. It later annexed the Golan Heights. The West Bank and Gaza were not annexed, but Israelis were given incentives to move there. It began establishing settlements in these areas. Since then, some of the settlements have grown and new ones are under construction, but some have been removed when Israel has withdrawn from the areas where they were built. The settlements are considered by many to be a source of contention as well as a roadblock in the peace process.

One central issue in the dispute has been the building of Israeli settlements.

WHAT ARE SETTLEMENTS?

Settlements are Israeli towns, villages, and cities that are located in what is considered by the Palestinians to be their territory. They are often enclosed by fences and gates, with armed guards patrolling the entrances. In 2017, there were 131 settlements in the West Bank, with approximately 385,000 Israeli settlers, as well as 97 outposts, which are settlements built without official permission.[1]

WEST BANK DIVISIONS

International law has defined three areas in the West Bank. Area C makes up about 60 percent of the West Bank, and it is entirely under Israeli control. About 40,000 Palestinians live there. The vast majority of Palestinians, almost 2 million, live in Areas A and B. Area B is jointly controlled by Israel and the Palestinian Authority and makes up about 20 percent of the West Bank. Area A is fully controlled by the Palestinian Authority and makes up the final 20 percent.[2] Most Palestinians in the West Bank live in Area A, which includes the major urban areas. Jewish people who try to visit this area are often attacked.

Israel did have additional settlements in the Gaza Strip and the Sinai Peninsula after it took control of those areas after the 1967 war, but it later dismantled them when it withdrew from Sinai in 1982 and from the Gaza Strip in 2005.

Israeli settlers have different reasons for living in these settlements. One is economic. The Israeli government offers subsidies and incentives for living in settlements, which are also often close to the settlers' places of employment. This contributes to a better quality of life for people in the settlements. Other settlers cite historical and religious reasons, saying that these areas are part of the biblical Israel and part of the Jewish birthright promised to them by God. However, even with these reasons, some Israelis and Jews in other parts of the world do not automatically think Jewish settlers should remain in these communities. They note that the settlements are expensive to build and maintain, and that they require constant protection by security forces. Many feel these costs are not worthwhile.

A SECURITY BARRIER

Security and safety for Israeli settlers in the occupied territories has been a great concern for the Israeli government. In 2002, the government of Israel approved the construction of a barrier wall in and around the West Bank to prevent violent attacks in Israel following a series of mass suicide bombings throughout the country. The wall is credited with having saved the lives of many Jewish, Muslim, and Christian Israelis.

FROM THE
HEADLINES

THE WEST BANK BARRIER

The construction of the West Bank Barrier by Israel has been controversial for its effect on Palestinians. In April 2016, construction resumed on a section of the barrier in Palestine, prompting a statement from the European Union saying that the body was "deeply concerned at the relaunch of works for the construction of the separation barrier in the Cremisan Valley. . . . Once built, the barrier will severely restrict access of almost 60 Palestinian families to their agricultural land and profoundly affect their livelihoods."[3]

Residents of a nearby Christian village had campaigned to the Israeli High Court in July 2015, urging them to cease construction, but the court ruled that the barrier is legitimate and allowed its construction to continue, noting that in the past, terrorists had moved through these areas to carry out attacks in West Jerusalem. When the network of fences, concrete walls, trenches, and closed military roads that make up the barrier is completed, it will take up approximately 7 percent of West Bank land. Previous routes for the barrier would have consumed 15 percent of the land, but petitions to the Israeli High Court moved the barrier line closer to the pre-1967 boundaries of Israel and Palestine.[4]

Palestinian protesters scaled the barrier in November 2009.

Some of the land for the barrier was taken from Palestinian landowners, although much of it follows the 1949 line dividing Israel and Palestine. However, in some cases, it split existing farmers' land or cut off their access to the land. The wall has also made it harder for some Palestinians to access services and resources, disrupted social and family life, made it difficult for some Palestinians to reach their workplaces, and made Palestinian territory even more fragmented. Approximately 65 percent of the proposed wall was completed by 2017. It will eventually be 440 miles (710 km) long. On July 9, 2004, the International Court of Justice (ICJ) issued an Advisory Opinion about the West Bank Barrier, saying that while Israel faced "indiscriminate and deadly acts of violence," the wall was a "violation of [Israel's] international obligations" and should be taken down.[5]

The West Bank Barrier has not only split Palestinians from each other but also has created an area known as the "seam zone" between the wall and the 1949 armistice line. Israel says the zone is necessary for security and to keep attackers from entering Israel from the West Bank. However, approximately 10,000 Palestinians live in the seam zone, and the UN estimates the number will grow to 30,000 once the barrier is completed.

THE PALESTINIAN VIEW

From a Palestinian viewpoint, the presence of Israeli settlements in the West Bank and East Jerusalem make it impossible for a future Palestinian state to exist in one large contiguous area.

FINISHING THE FENCE

Although the security fence is a source of dispute for Palestinians as far as boundaries and land access are concerned, every political party in Israel supports its completion. They cite an incident in June 2016, when 13-year-old Hallel Yaffa, who lived in the Israeli Kiryat Arba settlement in the West Bank, was stabbed to death in her bedroom by a Palestinian, 17-year-old Muhammad Tarayrah. He breached the settlement's own fence to access the girl's home. Israelis feel that the incident could have been prevented if the Israeli security fence construction had been completed.

Presently, Palestinian freedom of movement is already restricted by checkpoints, roadblocks, and other methods used to protect the Israeli settlements and Israel itself from militants and potential violence. Palestine often cites the settlements as an issue in peace talks, a point on which they are not willing to make concessions. Palestinian negotiators have agreed to such concessions in the past, but today's leaders have backtracked on such statements. Negotiators have stated that peace talks will only resume when Israel agrees to freeze the construction of new settlements.

The issue has also become more complicated with the election of President Donald Trump in 2016. He has stated that he strongly supports Israel, and he appointed an ambassador to Israel who supports settlements. His statement resulted in Israeli plans for thousands of new homes for settlers in these areas. President Trump requested that Israeli prime minister Netanyahu "hold back on settlements a bit," saying "we'll work something out," but his administration still does not view settlements as the central reason for the absence of peace in the area.[6]

RADICAL RESPONSES

Some Israeli youth have launched retaliation measures after the Israeli government's decisions to dismantle homes in the West Bank. The Hilltop Youth movement, a radical Israeli group, has been active for many years, building unauthorized Jewish outposts in the hills of the West Bank. Members build tiny camps with the hopes that they will grow and expand into thriving settlements with formal homes, schools, and roads. Some camps are named after Israeli settlers killed in terror attacks. This can elicit sympathy from Israelis, making the government more reluctant to take the camps down. Liat Weisel, a 19-year-old member of the Hilltop Youth, states:

We see [the Palestinians] as the occupiers. They are not supposed to be there. They have 22 [Arab] countries of their own. This is our land. The ideal situation is that they should leave.[7]

Young Israeli settlers protested against Palestinian statehood in 2011.

CHAPTER NINE

SEARCHING
FOR PEACE

Israel and Palestine have been in conflict since before Israel even became a state in 1948. They have gone through many governments and leaders, each with different approaches to finding a solution. As Israel passes its seventieth year of existence, what are the options for finding a compromise?

ONE STATE OR TWO?

When it comes to the future of Israel and Palestine, there are two simplified solutions that appear in the media frequently and are the focus of debates: the one-state solution and the two-state solution. The one-state solution holds that Israel and the Palestinian territories would become a single country. Palestinians

The many years of conflict have created thousands of innocent victims on both sides.

and Israelis would have equal rights, and the government would be a democracy. It would also designate Palestinians as refugees with a right of return.

While the one-state solution is often discussed as a viable option, it has had little support on the ground among Israelis and Palestinians. Both desire the right to self-determination and to have a state of their own. In addition, Israelis do not think they will be treated fairly as a minority population if Israel were to become another Muslim-majority country in the Middle East.

The two-state solution involves the creation of a separate Palestinian nation. The two-state solution has been supported by the United States, the UN, the PA, and Israel. Yet it also faces opposition from both the Israeli and Palestinian sides. Some Israelis are opposed because they believe that all biblical lands belong to the Jews.

"I BELIEVE THAT IN THE LONG RUN, SEPARATION BETWEEN ISRAEL AND THE PALESTINIANS IS THE BEST SOLUTION FOR RESOLVING THE ISRAELI-PALESTINIAN CONFLICT."[1]

—YITZHAK RABIN, PRIME MINISTER OF ISRAEL, 1993

Others think withdrawing from more land in order to create a Palestinian state would make Israel more vulnerable to terror attacks. While many Palestinians continue to agree in principle to Israel's right to exist and to the two-state solution, Palestinians have never officially agreed to support Israel as a Jewish homeland.

AT ISSUE

Even with the two-state solution being popular with both Israelis and Palestinians, as well as much of the rest of the world, there are issues involved that have prevented it from becoming the solution to the conflict. The first issue concerns the possible borders of the two new states. The two sides disagree on the best place to establish borders. One idea is to use the 1949 line. However, since Israel has built many settlements on land beyond these lines during the past five decades, this solution would likely involve dismantling some of these communities. In addition, this solution has been contested by Israel on security grounds. Many Israeli security experts argue that the 1949 armistice line would not provide Israel with defensible borders.

A HUNGER STRIKE

One of the many issues in the conflict is the rights of Palestinian prisoners in Israeli jails. In 2017, a group of prisoners argued for additional family visits and phone calls. They used a nonviolent form of protest, a hunger strike. Starting in April, they carried out their strike for 41 days. Many Palestinians looked up to the strikers as heroes for their actions. In May, Israel agreed to allow more family visits.

In 2017, at a joint appearance with Prime Minister Netanyahu, President Trump said, "I'm looking at two states and one state, and I like the one both parties like. I can live with either one."

The city of Jerusalem is another huge issue when it comes to creating two states. Both Israelis and Palestinians consider Jerusalem to be their capital, as well as a religious and cultural center. A two-state solution usually involves dividing the city between them, with the Israelis in the western part of the city and the Palestinians in the eastern portion. However, their respective holy sites aren't so easily divided. Many of them are in shared spaces. Israel has used more construction to assert its control over the entire city. Security is another key issue for both sides, as they try to protect their borders from attacks by radical groups. All these issues have stalled the implementation of a two-state solution.

It remains to be seen how the peace process will continue under changing US administrations. Many US presidents have tried to help Israel and Palestine find a solution that is fair to both peoples, but they have not been successful. President Trump's 2017 meeting with Israeli prime minister Netanyahu seemed to be hopeful, but the peace process has been dragging on for many years without success. Creating a workable solution for everyone will take enormous effort and cooperation.

ANOTHER JERUSALEM PROBLEM

Another issue concerning the city of Jerusalem has to do with the location of the US Embassy. A 1995 US law required the president to move the US Embassy from Tel Aviv to Jerusalem, but because of fears that the move would cause widespread hostility among Palestinians, every president since then has blocked the move. Both Clinton and Bush initially planned to move it, then decided not to. Israel is currently the only country where the US Embassy is not located in the city that has been designated by that country as its capital. President Trump, however, seems to want to change the situation. He said in a news conference, "I'd love to see that happen. We're looking at it very, very strongly. We're looking at it with great care," Trump said. "Great care, believe me, and we'll see what happens."[2]

ESSENTIAL
FACTS

MAJOR EVENTS

- 1920: The British Mandate gives the United Kingdom control of Palestine.

- 1948: Israel declares independence as a state.

- 1948-1949: The first Arab-Israeli War takes place.

- 1967: The Six-Day War between Israel, Egypt, Jordan, and Syria takes place.

- 1973: The Yom Kippur War is fought.

- 1978: The Camp David Accords are created.

- 1987: The First Intifada takes place.

- 2000: The Second Intifada takes place.

KEY PLAYERS

- Yasser Arafat, leader of the Palestine Liberation Organization from 1969 to 2004.

- Mahmoud Abbas, president of the Palestinian Authority from 2005–present.

- Yitzhak Rabin, prime minister of Israel from 1974–1977 and 1992–1995.

- Ariel Sharon, prime minister of Israel from 2001–2006.

- Benjamin Netanyahu, prime minister of Israel from 1996–1999 and from 2009–present.

IMPACT ON SOCIETY

The Israeli-Palestinian conflict has been a global issue since the founding of Israel in 1948, affecting peace in the Middle East. The conflict is based on which group, the Jews or the Palestinians, has the right to occupy what they each consider to be their ancestral homelands. It has also been the reason for war, violence, and terrorism in Israel, Palestine, Jordan, Egypt, and Syria since the advent of the Zionist movement of the late 1800s, and continues to cause conflict and diplomatic difficulties. As yet, there has been no successful plan for a peaceful resolution.

QUOTE

"My definition of a tragedy is a clash between right and right. And in this respect, the Israeli-Palestinian conflict has been a tragedy, a clash between one very powerful, very convincing, very painful claim over this land and another no less powerful, no less convincing claim."

—Israeli author Amos Oz

GLOSSARY

ACCORD
An official agreement, pact, or treaty.

ANNEX
To incorporate territory into a city, state, or country.

ANTI-SEMITISM
Hostility toward or prejudice against Jews.

CALIPH
A leader of an Islamic community.

CHECKPOINT
A barrier or manned gate, usually at a border, where travelers undergo security checks.

CONCENTRATION CAMP
A place where prisoners of war, political prisoners, or refugees are held in poor conditions and are forced to work.

GENERAL STRIKE

A strike that includes all workers in all industries within a city, region, or country.

MANDATE

An official order or commission to allow someone to do something.

PERSECUTE

To treat people cruelly or unfairly, especially because of their religious or spiritual beliefs or their race.

PILGRIMAGE

A long journey to a sacred place, to show devotion.

POGROM

An organized massacre of a particular ethnic or religious group, especially Jewish people.

SYNAGOGUE

The house of worship and communal center of a Jewish congregation.

TERRORISM

The illegal use of violence and intimidation against unarmed civilians, usually to accomplish a political goal.

ZIONISM

The global movement in support of self-determination for the Jewish people in their ancient homeland.

ADDITIONAL
RESOURCES

SELECTED BIBLIOGRAPHY

Dowty, Alan. *Israel/Palestine*. Malden, MA: Polity, 2012. Print.

Mansfield, Peter. *A History of the Middle East*, 4th edition. New York: Penguin, 2013. Print.

FURTHER READINGS

Farrell, Courtney. *Terror at the Munich Olympics*. Minneapolis, MN: Abdo, 2010. Print.

Immell, Myra. *The Creation of the State of Israel*. Detroit, MI: Greenhaven, 2010. Print.

Owings, Lisa. *Israel*. Minneapolis, MN: Abdo, 2013. Print.

ONLINE RESOURCES

To learn more about Israel and Palestine, visit
abdobooklinks.com. These links are routinely monitored and
updated to provide the most current information available.

MORE INFORMATION

For more information on this subject, contact or visit the
following organizations:

United Nations Visitor Center
Department of Public Information
United Nations Headquarters
760 United Nations Plaza
Room GA-1B-31
New York, NY 10017
212-963-4475
visit.un.org
The United Nations Visitor Center offers guided tours of the United
Nations and information about current worldwide events.

United States Holocaust Memorial Museum
100 Raoul Wallenberg Place SW
Washington, DC 20024-2126
202-488-0400
ushmm.org
The United States Holocaust Memorial Museum features exhibits that
memorialize the genocide carried out against Jews by Nazi Germany in
the 1930s and 1940s.

SOURCE
NOTES

CHAPTER 1. JUST ANOTHER DAY

1. Rachel Baruch. "What It's Like to Live in Israel Right Now." *World Post.* Huffington Post, n.d. Web. 9 Apr. 2017.

2. Sheren Khalel and Abed al Qaisi. "A Gruelling Life for Palestinian Workers in Israel." *Al Jazeera.* Al Jazeera, 6 Feb. 2016. Web. 15 Aug. 2017.

3. "Coping with Conflict: Israeli Author Amos Oz." *PBS NewsHour.* PBS, 23 Jan. 2002. Web. 15 Aug. 2017.

4. "Palestine Liberation Organization." *Permanent Observer Mission of the State of Palestine.* Permanent Observer Mission of the State of Palestine, 2017. Web. 10 Apr. 2017.

5. Einat Wilf. "An Israeli Leftist Finds Glimmer of Hope." *Israel Pulse.* Al Monitor, 6 Mar. 2014. Web. 15 Aug. 2017.

6. Sayed Kashua. "The Fruitless Israeli-Palestinian Discourse of Master and Servant." *Haaretz.* Haaretz, 12 Nov. 2015. Web. 15 Aug. 2017.

CHAPTER 2. A HOLY LAND

1. "1099: Jerusalem Captured in First Crusade." *History Channel.* History Channel, 2010. Web. 15 Aug. 2017.

2. Ibid.

CHAPTER 3. FORMING A NEW NATION

1. "What Was the British Mandate?" *ProCon.org.* ProCon.org, 26 June 2008. Web. 15 Aug. 2017.

2. "The Covenant of the League of Nations, Article 22." *Avalon Project.* Yale Law School, n.d. Web. 1 May 2017.

3. "1917: The Balfour Declaration." *This Day in History.* History Channel, 2009. Web. 15 Aug. 2017.

4. "The Palestine Mandate." *Avalon Project.* Yale Law School, n.d. Web. 1 May 2017.

5. Paul Halsall. "Modern History Sourcebook: Theodor Herzl: On the Jewish State, 1896." *Fordham University*. Fordham University, 1997. Web. 15 Aug. 2017.

6. James L. Gelvin. *The Israel-Palestine Conflict: One Hundred Years of War*, 3rd edition. New York: Cambridge UP, 2014. Print. 93.

7. "What Were the Arab Revolts of 1936–1939?" *ProCon.org*. ProCon.org, 14 May 2008. Web. 1 May 2017.

8. "British White Paper of 1939." *Avalon Project*. Yale Law School, 2008. Web. 15 May 2017.

9. James L. Gelvin. *The Israel-Palestine Conflict: One Hundred Years of War*, 3rd edition. New York: Cambridge UP, 2014. Print. 120–124.

10. Ofer Aderet. "The Forgotten Story of the Original Jaffa Oranges." *Haaretz*. Haaretz, 21 June 2015. Web. 15 Aug. 2017.

11. "Dates and Facts." *Embassy of Palestine, Rome, Italy*. Embassy of Palestine, 2017. Web. 15 Aug. 2017.

12. Ishaan Tharoor and Adam Taylor. "10 Quotes That Explain the History of the Gaza Conflict." *Washington Post*. Washington Post, 18 July 2014. Web. 15 Aug. 2017.

CHAPTER 4. THE VIEW FROM ISRAEL

1. William D. Rubenstein. "The Historiography of Rescue." *New York Times*. New York Times, 1997. Web. 15 Aug. 2017.

2. Mitchell Bard. "Pre-State Israel: Jewish Claim to the Land of Israel." *Jewish Virtual Library*. Jewish Virtual Library, n.d. Web. 6 May 2017.

3. "Declaration of Establishment of State of Israel." *Israel Ministry of Foreign Affairs*. Israel Ministry of Foreign Affairs, n.d. Web. 6 May 2017.

4. Edy Cohen. "There Was a Jewish Nakba, and It Was Even Bigger Than the Palestinian One." *Tower*. Tower, June 2016. Web. 15 Aug. 2017.

CHAPTER 5. THE VIEW FROM PALESTINE

1. "FAQ on the Nakba." *Institute for Middle East Understanding*. Institute for Middle East Understanding, 27 June 2012. Web. 15 Aug. 2017.

2. "Resolution 194." *United Nations Relief and Works Agency*. United Nations, n.d. Web. 8 May 2017.

3. Muhsin Yusuf. "The Partition of Palestine: An Arab Perspective." Palestine-Israel *Journal*. Middle East Publications, 2002. Web. 15 Aug. 2017.

4. "The Covenant of the Islamic Resistance Movement, 18 August 1988." *Avalon Project*. Yale Law School, n.d. Web. 1 July 2017.

SOURCE NOTES
CONTINUED

CHAPTER 6. INTERNATIONAL INVOLVEMENT

1. "Black September." *Encyclopedia.com.* International Encyclopedia of the Social Sciences, 2008. Web. 15 May 2017.

2. "Gaza Disengagement Plan: Text of the Sharon Plan (April 2004)." *Jewish Virtual Library.* Jewish Virtual Library, n.d. Web. 10 May 2017.

3. Steven Erlanger. "Tearfully but Forcefully, Israel Removes Gaza Settlers." *New York Times.* New York Times, 18 Aug. 2005. Web. 15 Aug. 2017.

4. "History of Mid-East Peace Talks." *BBC News.* BBC, 29 July 2013. Web. 15 Aug. 2017.

5. "Is Palestinian-Israeli Violence Being Driven by Social Media?" *BBC News.* BBC, 22 Oct. 2015. Web. 15 Aug. 2017.

6. Jeremy Diamond. "Trump Vows to Work as 'Mediator' for Israeli-Palestinian Peace." *CNN.* CNN, 3 May 2017. Web. 15 Aug. 2017.

CHAPTER 7. WAR, TERRORISM, AND SECURITY

1. "The 3 'No's of Khartoum." *Six-Day War.* CAMERA, 2007. Web. 1 July 2017.

2. Ibid.

3. "On This Day: December 9, 1987: Intifada begins on Gaza Strip." *History Channel.* History Channel, 2010. Web. 16 Aug. 2017.

4. "Intifada Toll 2000–2005." *BBC News.* BBC, 8 Feb. 2005. Web. 16 Aug. 2017.

5. "Al-Aqsa Intifada Timeline." *BBC News.* BBC, 29 Sept. 2004. Web. 16 Aug. 2017.

6. "Israel Defense Forces (IDF)." *Israel Ministry of Foreign Affairs.* Israel Ministry of Foreign Affairs, n.d. Web. 12 May 2017.

CHAPTER 8. THE SETTLEMENTS

1. Oren Liebermann. "What You Need to Know about the Israeli Settlements." *CNN*. CNN, 3 Feb. 2017. Web. 16 Aug. 2017.

2. Michael R. Fischbach. "The West Bank and Gaza: A Population Profile." *Population Reference Bureau*. PRB, Apr. 2002. Web. 16 Aug. 2017.

3. "EU 'Deeply Concerned' by New Phase of West Bank Barrier." *Times of Israel*. Times of Israel, 15 Apr. 2016. Web. 16 Aug. 2017.

4. Ibid.

5. "West Bank Barrier." *Occupied Palestinian Territory*. UN Office for the Coordination of Humanitarian Affairs, n.d. Web. 12 May 2017.

6. "Israel and the Palestinians: Can Settlement Issue Be Solved?" *BBC News*. BBC, 16 Feb. 2017. Web. 16 Aug. 2017.

7. Lulu Garcia-Navarro. "Israel Cracks Down on Radical 'Hilltop Youth.'" *NPR*. NPR, 9 Jan. 2012. Web. 16 Aug. 2017.

CHAPTER 9. SEARCHING FOR PEACE

1. Uri Dromi. "Yitzhak Rabin: A Statesman among Politicians." *Jewish Journal*. Jewish Journal, 29 Oct. 2015. Web. 16 Aug. 2017.

2. "Remarks by President Trump and Prime Minister Netanyahu of Israel in Joint Press Conference." *White House*. White House, 15 Feb. 2017. Web. 16 Aug. 2017.

INDEX

ABOUT THE
AUTHOR

Marcia Amidon Lusted has written more than 150 books and 600 magazine articles for young readers. She is also the former editor of *AppleSeeds* magazine, as well as a musician and permaculturist.